THE GREAT DANE CHRONICLES

Mr. Moose Caboose Finds his Way

by:- Johnathan Worden
Illustrated by:- Ayan Mansoori

I used to be so confused about who I was;
who I was supposed to be.

I realized from the time I was a little boy –
that I was very different.

I could feel it and I could definitely see it.

I could see that I was bigger than all the other boys and girls my age.

I could see the difference in my body.
I really stood out.
I couldn't hide any of it

The other boys' and girls' parents would pull them away from playing with me.

Sometimes they'd even cross the street to the other side – which really hurt the most.

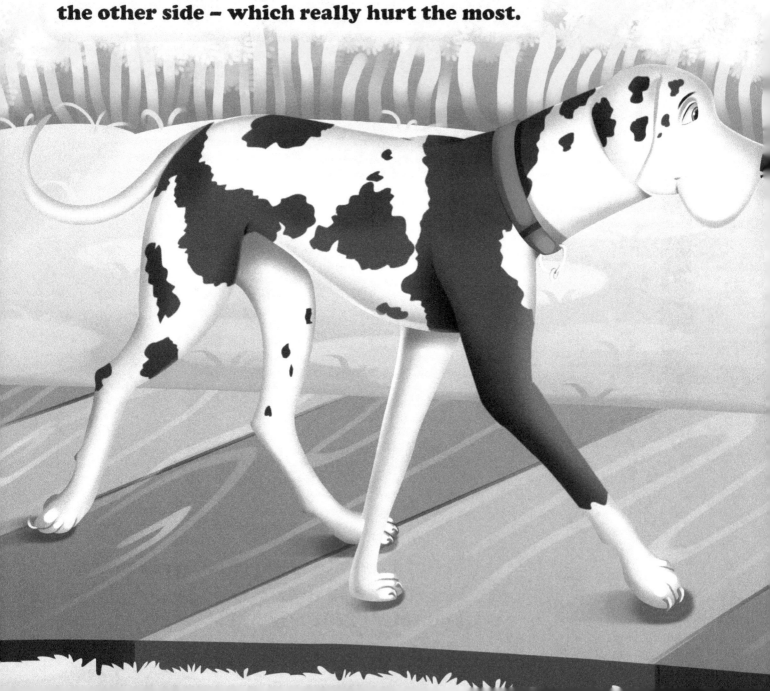

For some reason they always thought I was going to hurt them.

I could see it in their eyes.

My parents were different too.

My two dads always loved me and I could tell they just wanted the other boys and girls to accept me for who I was.

They made me feel better about my differences and loved me unconditionally.

They would say, "Everyone is just jealous about how fabulous you are!"

Maybe their parents weren't comfortable with my differences; so they kept their boys and girls away from me.

My parents knew how hard it could be to fit in; to feel it and to see it.

It made me feel better knowing I wasn't alone with my feelings.

The hardest part though, was that I didn't understand who I was, myself.

Starting with the way I looked, to my name, and where I was from – EVERYTHING was different than the way I felt inside.

I already told you that I was fairly large – in fact I thought I looked like a cow. People even said it to me – all the time.
I mean…I wasn't black, but I wasn't white – I was BOTH!

The hardest part is that I totes loved that about myself – and my parent did too.

They even have a little rhyme they sing to me that makes me warm inside and brightens my day...

"We always wanted a boy that looks like a cow...we ended up with you somehow."

Then there's my name... "Mr. Moose Caboose."
Now, I know I'm NOT a Moose, I don't even
have antlers!

For some reason though – I love my name! Sometimes they call me Moose, or Moosey, or Moose-arella-Cheesey... THAT'S my favorite one!

If you think that's a lot... how about where I'm from? I'm from Buffalo! Yikes – even more confusing!
I'm definitely not a Buffalo – I'm not even brown!

I've been saving the best part for last; and the hardest thing of all.
I'm a boy.
At least inside that's how I feel.
And my dad's just get it – they call me their funny boy all the time.

But on the outside – other's call me a dog.
I've just never felt like that was me.
I'M A BOY! And I'm shouting that on the
inside, but nobody can hear me.

Then one day everything changed...I got a
brother! His name is Duke.
We call him Dukey or Duka-doo!

He's JUST LIKE ME!
He's just as big.
He's black and white AND grey!

And now I'm not alone. I walk down the
street with my brother Duke– who's like
me...with my two Dad's.
I can see now that our differences make us
unique and beautiful.

I hear people say how cute we are, how adorable, how regal! I hear more of the positives than ever before.

I think those things were always there, but until I loved and accepted myself – I didn't hear them.
 I wouldn't want any other dad's in the world - and I know they wouldn't trade me for anything...

I'm Mr. Moose Caboose!
A boy, and a dog, that looks like a cow (not a moose), from Buffalo.
Now I'm comfortable in my own fur and proud to be me! After all – I'm like a snowflake and I'm one of a kind!

CPSIA information can be obtained
at www.ICGtesting.com
Printed in the USA
BVHW011207060721
611244BV00011B/116

9 780578 894249